The Poetry Of Jessie Pope

Jessie Pope was born in Leicester on March 18th 1868. Educated at North London Collegiate School and in her career became a regular contributor to Punch, The Daily Mail and The Daily Express, also writing for Vanity Fair, Pall Mall Magazine and the Windsor.

Jessie wrote extensively for children and had her verse published in Pope also wrote verse for many illustrated collections for children, including The Little Soldier Book (1907), Babes and Birds (1910), Babes and Beasts (1912), The Adventures of Silversuit (1912), Three Jolly Anglers (1913), Tom, Dick and Harry: their Deeds and Misdeeds (1914), and Frolicsome Friends (1915).

Her adult poetry is essentially patriotic and misses much of the carnage and brutality so powerfully portrayed by the War Poets.

She was extensively published by The Daily Mail in order to encourage enlistment among young men. Her simple rhymes and jingoistic stance encouraged many to sign up and fight for the Allies. During the war she published three volumes of verse; Jessie Pope's War Poems (1915), More War Poems (1915) and Simple Rhymes for Stirring Times (1916).

After the war, Pope continued to write poems, a novel and children's books. She married at age 61 in 1929 and moved from London to Fritton, near Great Yarmouth. Jessie Pope died on December, 14, 1941 in Devon.

Index Of Poems
"Bobs"
Silent Camp
War Girls
Play The Game
A Close Finish
Comrades In Arms-Lets
Marching To Germany
No!
Ware Wire!
A Muff
Love's Sacrifice
Snowflakes
A Cossack Charge
Who's For The Game?
Motor Martyrdom
Love In A Mist
Socks
Cobblers
A Humble Appeal
The Call
Loot!
Coo-ee
The Blackest Lie
Little And Good
A Royal Cracksman

De Wet
The Clerk Of The Weather
Three Jolly Huntsmen
Captive Conquerors
Lights Out
The War Budget
The Zeppelin Armada
A Valentine [From an old Lover]
Crumbs Of Comfort
To A Stout Shepherdess
The Comet
The Two Goliaths
An Overlord
April Antidotes
The Outpost
To A Taube
A Sing-Song
An Anzac Cap
Anzac
An Anzac Poem
The K A Boys
Another Pair Of Sleeves
A Sore Point
The Niggers
The Knitting Song
The Longest Odds
The Nut
The Nut's Birthday
A Vain Appeal
April Antidotes
The Lads Of The Maple Leaf
The Call Of The Congo
Captain Von Muller

"Bobs"
The call came in the stormy night,
Beneath a stranger's sky.
The soldier of a life-long fight,
Still fighting, went to die.

His country's honour was his goal;
Patient, unswerving, brave,
His mind, his heart, his work, his soul
His very all, he gave.

He toiled to rouse us from our sleep,
And now he takes his rest,
And we it is not ours to weep,

But follow his behest.

'Tis ours to make this matter plain
That though our 'Bobs' has gone,
Though dust returns to dust again
His soul goes marching on.

Silent Camp

In heaven, a pale uncertain star,
Through sullen vapour peeps,
On earth, extended wide and far,
In all the symmetry of war,
A weary army sleeps.

The heavy-hearted pall of night
Obliterates the lines,
Save where a dying camp-fire's light
Leaps up and flares, a moment bright,
Then once again declines.

Black, solemn peace is brooding low,
Peace, still unbroken, when
There comes a sound, an ebb and flow—
The steady breathing, deep and slow,
Of half-a-million men.

The pregnant dawn is drawing nigh,
The dawn of power or pain ;
But now, beneath the mournful sky,
In sleep's maternal arms they lie
Like children once again.

War Girls

'There's the girl who clips your ticket for the train,
And the girl who speeds the lift from floor to floor,
There's the girl who does a milk-round in the rain,
And the girl who calls for orders at your door.
Strong, sensible, and fit,
They're out to show their grit,
And tackle jobs with energy and knack.
No longer caged and penned up,
They're going to keep their end up
'Til the khaki soldier boys come marching back.

There's the motor girl who drives a heavy van,
There's the butcher girl who brings your joint of meat,
There's the girl who calls 'All fares please!' like a man,
And the girl who whistles taxi's up the street.
Beneath each uniform

Beats a heart that's soft and warm,
Though of canny mother-wit they show no lack;
But a solemn statement this is,
They've no time for love and kisses
Till the khaki soldier boys come marching back.

Play The Game
Twenty-Two stalwarts in stripes and shorts
Kicking a ball along,
Set in a square of leather-lunged sports
Twenty-two thousand strong,
Some of them shabby, some of them spruce,
Savagely clamorous all,
Hurling endearments, advice or abuse,
At the muscular boys on the ball.

Stark and stiff 'neath a stranger's sky
A few hundred miles away,
War-worn, khaki-clad figures lie,
Their faces rigid and grey
Stagger and drop where the bullets swarm,
Where the shrapnel is bursting loud,
Die, to keep England safe and warm
For a vigorous football crowd !

Football's a sport, and a rare sport too,
Don't make it a source of shame.
To-day there are worthier things to do.
Englishmen, play the game!
A truce to the League, a truce to the Cup,
Get to work with a gun,
When our country's at war we must all back up
It's the only thing to be done!

A Close Finish
['A marriage is arranged between Miss Diana Dashington and Lord Broadacres.']

The race of the season is over ;
I've lost and Diana has won ;
She's feasting on Broadacres' clover,
And I am right out of the fun.
Though Di was the one to begin it,
She soon found me making the pace ;
I thought all along I should win it,
And only backed her for a place.

At Ascot Diana was leading,
At Henley I spurted ahead ;
At Cowes side by side we were speeding;

At Trouville I fancy I led.
Neck to neck we ran, shoulder to shoulder,
The pack was too killing to last
(If the weather had only been colder!)
I flagged, and Diana shot past.

My heart's not by any means broken;
I hope I'm not wanting in pluck ;
A tear or two, low be it spoken,
Then I kissed her and wished her good luck.
Di won the race fairly as stated;
But when her attractions are reckoned,
My own must not be underrated
I finished a very good second!

Comrades In Arms-Lets
Not theirs the popular uniform
That takes the feminine heart by storm,
And wins soft glances, shy or warm,
The perquisites of pluck.
But theirs the commonplace city kit,
With a blue and white stripe round the sleeve of it,
And a stout little truncheon to do the trick,
If ever they have the luck.

Not theirs to fight on the Allies' wing,
Or even to march with soldierly swing,
While the people are cheering like anything,
To the stirring roll of drums.
But theirs to stand 'neath a pitchy sky.
On a lonely beat, with a vigilant eye
For the skulking shape of a German spy
Who bother him ! never comes.

By night they guard though possibly bored
Those places where light and water are stored,
And since the family can't be ignored
Business as usual by day.
Though sport may be scanty compared with the blanks,
They're doing their level, the armletted ranks,
With no expectation of ha'pence or thanks,
For that is the S.C.'s way.

Marching To Germany
Swing along together, lads ; we'll have a little song,
Kits won't be so heavy and the way won't be so long.
We're goin' to cook ' the Sossiges,' to cook 'em hot and strong
While we go marching to Germany.

Chorus

Hurrah, hurrah, for Berlin on the Spree !
Hurrah, hurrah, there's 'Sossiges' for tea!
We're out to catch the Kaiser and bring him to his knee
While we go marching to Germany.

How the girls all love us as they see us marching by!
Some of them are saucy ones, and some of them are shy.
Guess they know we're cold and wet to keep them warm and dry
While we go marching to Germany.

Chorus

What about the slacker chaps, who look before they leap?
Lads who like to save their skins and have their proper sleep
Let them put on petticoats and feel a little cheap,
While we go marching to Germany.

Chorus

Britain's little Army can be swept away like fluff;
That's the Kaiser's fairy tale ice we'll give the beggars snuff ;
Rattle 'em and bustle 'em, and make 'em shout 'Enough!'
While we go marching to Germany.

Chorus

Hurrah, hurrah, for Berlin on the Spree!
Hurrah, hurrah, there's 'Sossiges' for tea!
We're out to catch the Kaiser and to bring him to his knee,
While we go marching to Germany.

No!
By bridge and battery, town and trench,
They're fighting with bull-dog pluck;
Not one, from Tommy to General French,
Is down upon his luck.
There are some who stand and some who fall,
But how does the chorus go
That echoing chant in the hearts of all?
'Are we downhearted? NO!'
There's Jack, God bless him, upon the foam,
His isn't an easy task,
To strike for England, to strike right home,
So much, no more, does he ask.
On the dreadnought's deck where the big guns bark,
Or in quiet depths below
The salt wind wafts us a chantey. Hark !

' Are we downhearted ? NO !'

And what of the girl who is left behind,
And the wife who misses her mate ?
Oh, well, we've got our business to mind
Though it's only to watch and wait.
So we'll take what comes with a gallant heart
As we busily knit and sew,
Trying, God help us, to do our part,
' Are we downhearted ? NO !'

Ware Wire!
When the beagles are running like steam,
When the plough is as sticky as glue,
When the scent is an absolute scream,
And there's wire in the fence to get through
Who waits to look after his pal ?
Hung up? then he's out of the fun.
Torn, muddy, and blown, every man on his own
That's the time-honoured rule of the run.

There's wire in the fences of France.
There are bullets that whistle and spit.
The word goes along to advance,
And the wire clutches somebody's kit.
' Hold hard ! I'll unhook you, old chap.
No hurry. Oh, rubbish What rot!'
Shots patter and thud, shells burst in the mud.
' Don't pull ! Now, you're clear no, you're not!'

Well, that is how the business is done.
A sportsman will brook no delay,
With hounds it's life and death run,
He's out for himself all the way.
But when black Eternity gapes
There's time and there's patience enough.
A case of 'ware wire, and a pal under fire
' No hurry ' that's British-made stuff !

A Muff
I wanted a muff
On an up-to-date scale,
Of some soft fluffy stuff,
With a head and a tail;
So simple and innocent-hearted
I started to go to a sale.

My muscles are tough,
I'm not sickly or pale;

But that shop was enough
To make 'Hercules' quail.
The ladies were snatching and gripping,
Each using her arm like a flail.

My passage was rough
And as slow as a snail.
In attempting to luff
I was pinned to a bale,
And asked 'to mind where I was pushing"
By a frowsy and frenzied female.

They ruined my ruff
And twitched off my veil;
The shopman was bluff
When I told him my tale,
And I vowed the next time I played football
I would wear a costume of chain mail.

I went home in a huff,
Looking feeble and frail,
Still minus a muff
With a head and a tail
But my brother politely informed me
I was one, to go to a sale.

Love's Sacrifice

When I asked my dear Edwin to shave
I'd never a thought of denial;
He'd been such an absolute slave,
I put his devotion on trial.
But his eye threw a sinister dart,
His features grew dogged and grave ;
Still I hardly expected to part
When I asked him to shave.

He refused, and seemed eager to jest,
Till he saw my determined expression.
A moustache, he said, suited him best,
And helped in his budding profession.
' What! Like yours' I replied with a sneer.
He smiled when my temper grew hot,
And when I indulged in a tear
He said, ' Certainly not.'

'Twas enough, and I said what I felt,
Indignant and adamant-hearted,
On some of his drawbacks I dwelt
He took up his hat and departed.
I waited and waited in vain.

Disconsolate, haggard and white,
I wrestled each day with my pain
Till Saturday night.

Then I wrote and confessed I was wrong,
My hand with emotion was shaking,
I prayed him to come before long
To the heart that was his and was breaking.
Three terrible hours did I wait ;
He came and my reason was saved.
Then I saw what had made him so late
My Edwin had shaved.

Snowflakes
A little curly-headed god
Through asphodel came creeping,
Found Mother Juno on the nod,
And safely slipped her keeping.
Away he frolicked, full of mirth,
Until he glanced in pity
Upon the muddiness of earth,
The squalour of the city.

His flashing pinions forth he spread,
And flew with dart and quiver
To a celestial garden bed
Beside a sapphire river.
To deck the dingy world down there
He stripped each dazzling flower,
And flung through the cerulean air
The petals in a shower.

His treasured blossoms fluttered down,
He watched them softly falling,
Until, alas! they reached the town
Where men and carts were crawling.
Before the city's fevered fumes
They sank in helpless flutter,
And men came out with spades and brooms
And swept them in the gutter.

A Cossack Charge
Cossacks they're coming!
The eager hoofs are drumming,
On glinting steel the autumn sunlight glances.
The distant mass draws nearer,
The surging line shows clearer
An angry, tossing wave of manes and lances.

The torrent opens wider;
As one, move horse and rider,
One heart, one soul, one body, and one breath.
The narrow eyes are laughing,
The wine of war they're quaffing,
The glorious draught of swift, resistless death.

They've met them they're through them !
In writhing heaps they strew them,
Through breaking lines the whipping whirlwind crashes.
Then pauselessly it flies on
Away to the horizon,
And disappears in distant, glinting flashes.

Who's For The Game?
Who's for the game, the biggest that's played,
The red crashing game of a fight?
Who'll grip and tackle the job unafraid?
And who thinks he'd rather sit tight?
Who'll toe the line for the signal to 'Go!'?
Who'll give his country a hand?
Who wants a turn to himself in the show?
And who wants a seat in the stand?
Who knows it won't be a picnic – not much-
Yet eagerly shoulders a gun?
Who would much rather come back with a crutch
Than lie low and be out of the fun?
Come along, lads
But you'll come on all right
For there's only one course to pursue,
Your country is up to her neck in a fight,
And she's looking and calling for you.

Motor Martyrdom
I never have clung to a motor car,
Or crouched on a motor bike.
Worry and scurry, clank and jar
I cordially dislike.

I do not care for grimy hair,
For engines that explode,
But of one and all I've the put and call,
For I live on the Ripley Road.

I drank the country breeze at first,
Unsoiled by fetid fumes,
But now I am cursed with a constant thirst
That parches and consumes.

I am choked and hit with smoke and grit
When I venture from my abode;
My pets are maimed and my eyes inflamed,
For I live on the Ripley Road.

I pass my days in a yellow fog,
My nights in a dreadful dream,
Haunted by handlebar, clutch and cog,
And eyes that goggle and gleam.

I am not robust, but I dine on dust
Gratuitously bestowed,
And for twopence I'll sell my house in the dell
By the side of the Ripley Road.

Love In A Mist
Beneath an Ilfracombe machine,
While thunderstorms were raging,
Strephon and Chloe found the scene
Exceedingly engaging;
Though Mother Earth reproached the skies
With flinging pailfuls at her,
When Strephon looked in Chloe's eyes
The weather didn't matter.

When 'Arry up on 'Ampstead 'Eath
Performed a double shuffle,
The rain above, the mud beneath,
His spirits failed to ruffle;
For 'Arriet was by his side
In maddened mazes whirling
And little cared his promised bride
To see her plumes uncurling.

For one resplendent Summer morn
Young Edwin fondly waited,
Till Angelina grew forlorn
And quite emaciated.
When Hampton Court was like a sponge,
With mists their way beguiling,
He seized her hand and took the plunge,
And came up wet and smiling.

Socks
Shining pins that dart and click
In the fireside's sheltered peace
Check the thoughts the cluster thick -

20 plain and then decrease.

He was brave – well, so was I
Keen and merry, but his lip
Quivered when he said good-bye

Purl the seam-stitch, purl and slip.

Never used to living rough,
Lots of things he'd got to learn;
Wonder if he's warm enough

Knit 2, catch 2, knit, turn.

Hark! The paper-boys again!
Wish that shout could be suppressed;
Keeps one always on the strain

Knit off 9, and slip the rest.

Wonder if he's fighting now,
What he's done an' where he's been;
He'll come out on top somehow

Slip 1, knit 2, purl 14.

Cobblers
They were "cobbers," that's Anzac for chum.
But it means rather more than we mean
A friendship that will not succumb,
Though distance or death intervene.
Adventure, success, and mishap
In boyhood they'd shared, so no wonder
They jumped at the chance of a scrap
And booked with the crowd from "down under."

In a narrow Gallipoli trench
They chanced upon glimpses of hell,
And a thirst there was nothing to quench
But a deluging downpour of shell;
Perpetual ridges they took,
They charged and they cursed and they shouted,
But nothing their recklessness shook
Till one of the "cobbers" got "outed."

The other one came back at night,
Exhausted in body and brain,
And groped round the scene of the fight,
But sought for his "cobber" in vain.

His spirit was heavy with grief,
His outlook was sombre and blotted,
But his bayonet brought him relief
Next, morning — and that's when he "got it."

Scene: Midday, Victoria street,
An Anzac (in blue) on each side
A coo-ee, wild, ringing, and sweet
The taxicabs swerve and divide.
For traffic they don't care a toss,
There, right in the middle, they're meeting;
Stay, let's draw a curtain across
Where the two long-lost "cobbers" are greeting.

A Humble Appeal
She was a pretty, nicely mannered mare,
The children's pet, the master's pride and care,
Until a man in khaki came one day,
Looked at her teeth, and hurried her away.

With other horses packed into a train
She hungered for her master's voice in vain;
And later, led 'twixt planks that scare and slip,
They slung her, terrified, on board a ship.

Next came, where thumps and throbbing filled the air,
Her first experience of mal de mare;
And when that oscillating trip was done
They hitched her up in traces to a gun.

She worked and pulled and sweated with the best;
A stranger now her glossy coat caressed
Till flashing thunderstorms came bursting round
And spitting leaden hail bestrewed the ground.

With quivering limbs, and silky ears laid back,
She feels a shock succeed a sharper crack,
And, whinnying her pitiful surprise,
Staggers and falls, and tries in vain to rise.

Alone, forsaken, on a foreign field
What moral does this little record yield?
Who tends the wounded horses in the war?
Well that is what the Blue Cross League is for.

The Call
Who's for the trench
Are you, my laddie?
Who'll follow French

Will you, my laddie?
Who's fretting to begin,
Who's going out to win?
And who wants to save his skin-
Do you, my laddie?

Who's for the khaki suit
Are you, my laddie?
Who longs to charge and shoot
Do you, my laddie?
Who's keen on getting fit,
Who means to show his grit,
And who'd rather wait a bit
Would you, my laddie?

Who'll earn the Empire's thanks-
Will you, my laddie?
Who'll swell the victor's ranks
Will you, my laddie?
When that procession comes,
Banners and rolling drums
Who'll stand and bite his thumbs-
Will you, my laddie?

Loot!
When Blucher helped us make an end
Of Bonaparte, the common foe,
He came to England as a friend,
About a hundred years ago.
The sight of London fired his breast,
He gazed with eagerness and wonder,
And, brimming with Teutonic zest,
He cried, 'Oh, what a town to plunder! '

Der Tag, however, was not yet.
A century has passed away.
Blucher has settled Nature's debt,
But his example lives to-day
And kindles in the German mind
An altar that there's no uprooting,
Where love of power is enshrined,
Together with a love of looting.

They spoil and pillage, smash and swill;
And helpless cities they have racked
Must, willy nilly, pay the bill
For the delight of being sacked,
That motto 'Blood and Iron' is done;
A newer one must be enscrolled;

The carte de visite of the Hun
Should now be printed, ' Blood and Gold.'

Coo-ee
"Down under" boys on furlough are in town
Discharged from hospital, repaired and braced,
Their faces still retain, their native brown,
Their millinery captivates our taste.

They've proved themselves a terror to the Turk,
Of cut and thrust they bear full many a token,
But though they've been through grim, heartbreaking work,
The Anzac spirit never can be broken.

Their talk is picturesque, their manner frank,
A little hasty, what they think— they say
They've got a down on arrogance and swank,
Passive submission doesn't come their way.

Risk and adventure are their fondest joys,
If there's a fight around, well, they'll be in it
To tell the truth, they really are "some" boys
You get quite friendly with them in a minute.

Quite friendly, yes, no harm in being friends,
They must not find their furlough dull and tame,
But, girls, see to it there the matter ends,
And show that London girls can play the game,

While of good comradeship you take your fill
Don't use your power to make their hearts your plunder,
But let them pause, and hear when nights are still
The other girl who coo-ees from "down under."

The Blackest Lie
Big bully Belgium,
Breathing blood and flame,
Crafty as a serpent
In a cunning game,
Sent a note to England,
Sent a note to France,
'Let us crush the Fatherland
While we have the chance!'

Poor little Germany,
Gentle land of peace,
Seeking the Millennium,
When armaments shall cease;
Rather grieved than angry,

Called her sons to fight,
To protect their Fatherland,
As was only right.

Hurry with the whitewash,
Pour it out in streams!
Bleach the ravaged country,
Louvain, Antwerp, Rheims!
Belgium concocted war,
Thus deserves her fate!
That's the blackest Teuton lie
Published up to date.

Little And Good

Young Thompson was a bit too short,
But hard as nails and level-headed,
And in his soul the proper sort
Of dogged pluck was deeply bedded;
To join the ranks he almost ran,
But saw the weedy supersede him;
Though he was every inch a man,
His country didn't need him.

He read each passionate appeal
On wall and window, cab and cart;
How impotent they made him feel !
He tried once more, though sick at heart.
In vain ! He saw the sergeants smirk;
He argued, but they would not heed him;
So sullenly trudged back to work
His country didn't need him.

But, now the standard height's curtailed,
Again he goes to join the ranks;
Though yesterday he tried and failed
To-day they welcome him with thanks.
Apparently, he's just as small,
But since his size no more impedes him,
In spirit he is six foot tall
Because his country needs him.

A Royal Cracksman

When the housebreaking business is slack
And cracksmen are finding it slow
For all the sea-siders are back
And a great many more didn't go
Here's excellent news from the front
And joy in ;
Things are looking up since

The German Crown Prince
Has been giving a fillip to trade.

His methods are quite up-to-date,
Displaying adroitness and dash;
What he wants he collects in a crate,
What he doesn't he's careful to smash.
An historical chateau in France
With Imperial ardour he loots,
Annexing the best
And erasing the rest
With the heels of his soldierly boots.

Sikes reads the report with applause,
It's quite an inspiring affair;
But a sudden idea gives him pause
The Germans must stop over there!
So he flutters a Union Jack
To help to keep Englishmen steady,
Remarking, ' His nibs
Mustn't crack English cribs,
The profession is crowded already.'

De Wet

Foe and friend and foe again,
Turning coat and turning yet,
That's a feat you don't disdain,
De Wet.

England's easy, England's kind,
Quick to pardon and forget.
There's a limit, as you'll find,
De Wet.

Glad to raise a fallen foe,
Ready to erase a debt.
Quick to spare a traitor? No,
De Wet.

England trusts a solemn vow,
That's her way. We don't regret.
So be it, we know you now,
De Wet.

Treachery will miss its aim,
You'll be learning, never fret.
That it's best to play the game,
De Wet.

The Clerk Of The Weather
Re: HEAT WAVE

Dear Sir, we've had enough.
Do you forget, I think you do, perhaps,
Our temperate position on the maps?
Daily we mourn the collar's swift collapse,
The limp and wrinkled cuff.

Dear Sir, we've got to work.
We cannot all lie idle on the beach,
Or skim, white- winged, the river's limpid reach.
We've got to buy and sell, to talk and teach,
Although we'd like to shirk.

Think of the crowded street,
The roar, the clatter, and the throbbing head
Where shout and clash, and jangle meet and spread,
And thought is irksome and the brain is lead
And asphalt grills the feet.

Now don't get in a huff.
Pity the pain the stifling town endures,
A bracing rain will work a thousand cures.
Believe me, Sir, obediently yours
P.S. We've had enough.

Three Jolly Huntsmen
Three jolly, old huntsmen, Joe, Jerry, Jim,
Took lunch at 'The Three Cornered Hat';
Now Jerry was lanky, but Joe wasn't slim,
And Jim was delightfully fat.

They sat at the table and worked with a will
At all the good things spread about them ;
They munched and they crunched and they gobbled, until
The hunt started gaily without them.

Joe cried 'Hoity Toity! Alack! and Confound!'
Jim moaned, ' Let's complain to the Police!'
But Jerry remarked 'I've an old basset hound,
And you chaps have a puppy a-piece;

'A hunt on our own is our only resource!'
With rapture the hounds started yelping.
While each huntsman proceeded to climb on his horse,
The ostlers and stable-boys helping.

The basset hound soon found a scent to his taste;
He gave tongue and was off like a shot,

Behind him the pups and the hunting men raced,
For the pace was exceedingly hot.

But a garden of flower-beds, all bordered with box,
Put an end to their sporting excursion;
For the riotous pack was not hunting a fox.
But Lady Polpero's pet Persian.

Jim and Jerry leaped back to the road whence they came,
Joe lingered to whip off the hounds;
Then he tried to escape from the furious dame,
But lost his way out of the grounds.

She made her men seek him with furious shout;
But he finally managed to thwart her.
By crouching, with only his nose sticking out.
In a water-butt, brimful of water.

Now Jim on his dappled mare sturdily sat,
And trotted once more down the street,
And he said, 'Well, there's this about hunting a cat.
It makes me want something to eat!'

He bought half a chicken to gnaw on the way.
And filled up his flask with brown sherry.
Then, lighting a weed, without further de-lay.
He cantered away after Jerry.

This flask he was taking a leisurely pull,
When he heard a loud roar in the rear,
And, turning, discovered a brisk looking bull
Drawing most disconcertingly near.

His Dapple was munching a tuft of sweet grass,
And when urged to 'gee hup!' she refused to;
So Joe had to run on his own legs, alas!
At a pace that they'd never been used to.

Why,' whimpered Jim, 'am I hunting in pink?
It is a colour these savage brutes love!'
And he prayed as he raced, through the ground he might sink
And leave his pursuer above.

Two yokels ran up and showed wonderful sense
In using their forks as a lever,
And hooked the stout runaway over the fence,
While the bull took it out of his beaver.

Now Jerry till sundown continued the chase,
With his basset hound working a line
Which led them at last to a desolate place.

Thank goodness the weather was fine!

Beneath a gnarled oak tree they came to halt,
For there crouched a furry white Madam;
Which proved that their hunting once more was at fault.
And again had the Persian cat 'had 'em'.

Puss swore with such spite, they were glad to retire,
By a pony track over the moor;
But what with the boulders, the gorse, and the mire.
Their progress was painfully poor.

Till Jerry, half-famished, endeavoured to jog
Down a track that grew thinner and thinner.
And finally, taking a toss in a bog.
Had a mouthful of mud for his dinner.

E'd never been quite so unlucky before,
To the best of his honest belief,
And still he'd another adventure in store;
For some rustics were chasing a thief.

In the dusk they were quite convinced Jerry was he,
And captured the horse he was riding.
While the huntsman crouched down by the stump of a tree
To secure and escape from a hiding.

That night in the bar of 'The Three Cornered Hat'
He ran his two cronies to earth,
And his plight was so mournful and woe-begone, that
The rafters resounded with mirth.

Then, snug by the fire, with their toddy at hand.
While the Landlady mended their tatters.
They declared, one and all, that the sport had been grand
And, after all, nothing else matters!

Captive Conquerors

Oh! Stuttgart Frauleins, and capacious Fraus,
What shocking news is this that filters through?
Have you been fostering domestic rows
By casting, naughtily, glad eyes of blue
At poor old Tommy in his prison-house?
Tut! tut! This is a pretty how-d'ye do!

Anna and Gretchen, where's your strength of mind?
Think of that khaki crowd whose force of arms
Bustles your goose-step legions from behind ;
These very captives should inspire alarms.
You are indeed disloyal and unkind .

To fall a prey to their dishevelled charms.
The gods have come among you, I admit,
To make your jealous Herren fume and fuss.
Unkempt, unshaven, rather short of kit,
The prisoners attract you even thus.
But, Fraus and Frauleins, what's the use of it?
Their hearts, please understand, belong to us!

Lights Out
Darkness expectant, discreet
Only a lamp here and there,
Gloom in the clattering street,
Stygian black in the square;
Dazzling fascias and fronts,
Scintillant sky-scrapers banished,
Snuffed and shut down are the spangles of Town.
London has vanished.

Only a few months ago
London woke up every night;
Dances or 'Chemin' or Show,
Festival vistas of light.
Everywhere glitter and glare,
Junket and revelry keeping.
Yes, but despite the laughter and light,
London was sleeping.

Searchlights are probing the skies,
Eastward their streamers are trailed ;
Masked are the city's bright eyes
Even the tramcars are veiled.
Cockneys turn in at eleven,
'Stop Press' thirst finally slaked.
Turn the lights out. Now, without doubt,
London's awake!

The War Budget
Hodge waded through the weekly news,
'The Income Tax, he said,
'That's nowt to me, I shallunt lose,
'Twill hit the boss instead.
Lloyd George he be the man for I,
Us poor have nowt to fear.'
He paused then gave a dismal cry:
' They're goin' to tax my beer'

' A good thing too!' replied his wife.
' 'Twill keep you from the pub,

Swilling each evening of your life,
While I work at the tub!'
Across the inglenook she reached,
The welcome news to see,
Then, in resentful clamour, screeched:
'3d. a pound on tea'

MORAL

To foot the bill it's only fair
That everyone should do their share,
And since we all are served the same,
Pay and look pleasant that's the game.

The Zeppelin Armada
'To-day, since Zeppelins are in the air,
And folks glance skywards as they go their ways,
Let us hark back a bit to an affair
That happened in Queen Bess's sturdy days,
When the Armada, backed by Spanish lust
A fleet that floating palaces resembled
Sailed proudly forth to crush us in the dust,
While all the tremulous in England trembled.

What was the fate of those unwieldy craft?
Our little frigates made of British oak
Harassed the mighty galleons fore and aft,
Handy to strike and shun the counterstroke.
The Great Invasion ended in defeat.
No more could Philip play the part of mocker,
The rout of the Armada was complete,
And down it went to Davy Jones's locker.

What frigates did in 1558
May be repeated in the air to-day,
When clumsy Zeppelins may meet their fate
From aeroplanes that sting and dart away.
A well-equipped and handy air patrol
Would circumvent an aerial attack.
If London is to be the Zeppes' goal,
It's up to us to see they don't go back!

A Valentine [From an old Lover]
Estelle, when you and I were rising nine
Perhaps you'd rather I suppressed the date
I spent a shilling on a valentine
And left it for you at the garden gate.
Therein my heart was imaged in a bower
Of tinsel roses, with a tender verse on;

I followed it in less than half an hour
Impatient for your gratitude in person.

You ran and kissed my cheek with candied lips,
A habit, by the way, you've since neglected;
You gambolled up and down in little skips,
Yet failed to do the thing that I expected.
It should have been a give-and-take affair;
You had my tinsel heart, while I had not one,
And when I asked for yours, to make it square,
You playfully remarked you hadn't got one.

I was appalled my little bosom heaved
Such disappointment did not seem correct.
With rising tears I felt myself deceived
And lost my temper at your base neglect.
'I'll have mine back I paid for it, it's mine!'
I cried. We fought and tore the paper frilling.
By dint of nail you kept that valentine,
And left me howling for my wasted shilling.

Since then how many years have slipped away?
And time has tamed my temper to submission.
You're tall and dignified, and yet to-day
I find myself in just the same position.
The heart from out my bosom you've decoyed,
Though day by day with strenuous endeavour
I would recall it to its aching void.
I strive in vain my heart is yours for ever.

Crumbs Of Comfort
When Gladys comes a whisper wakes,
A sudden thrill prevails,
She holds the eyes of men, and takes
The wind out of our sails.
In spite of every art we use,
Their bosoms she transfixes,
And yet I'm glad to know her shoes
Are unromantic sixes.

The frocks that Leonora wears
Are absolutely sweet,
She practices such Frenchy airs
It's hopeless to compete.
Her lace is fine, her silks are thick,
Her sables make one sicken;
And yet, though Leonora's chic,
She's certainly no chicken.

Diana has a sporting bent

And not a little side,
She's hot upon a screamin' scent
And knows the way to ride.
Her doggy tendencies would please
A print like Mr. Strachey's,
But, though she drops her final

To A Stout Shepherdess
Dear lady, are you open to a hint
As down our sober pavement you display
A costume reminiscent of a print
Of Valenciennes and shepherdesses gay?
When Watteau, master of Rococo art,
Depicted nymphs in pastoral disguises,
His cunning pencil only could impart
A charm to graceful shapes and slender sizes.

That saucy Watteau hat where rosebuds twine
Is not the sort a florid dame should wear.
Although tip-tilted at the proper line
Upon your own, or someone else's, hair.
Those panniers of Pompadour brocade,
That scanty skirt, although no doubt de rigueur,
That corsage laced, with ruffles overlaid,
Are not, I think, intended for your figure.

Go home, dear lady, lay your gauds aside,
Afflict no more your feet with Louis heels,
Wear ample garments, flowing, full and wide
Take my advice, and see how nice it feels.
Accommodate your features with a veil,
And let your hat be quietly trimmed, and shady:
Then, though as shepherdess you frankly fail,
You may be more successful as a lady.

The Comet
Last week we started out in glee,
The boys and Bertha, Aunt and me,
Across the village green to see
The comet;
Some people really must be blind,
Or only give it half their mind,
It isn't difficult to find
Far from it.

Jack found one in ' The Lady's Chair,'
And Bertha, with her nose in air,
Described a couple in ' The Bear '
I backed her;

While Auntie, dazzled by the view,
Stepped in the ditch before she knew,
It took us twenty minutes to
Extract her.

With stars and comets on the brain
Two figures vanished up the lane,
A better view of course to gain,
But whether
It was that Auntie missed her sleep
Or found the lane a trifle steep,
She sulked, because we would not keep
Together.

We found the others looking black,
But though they made a joint attack,
Their thrusts we managed back to back-
To parry;
They voted finding comets slow,
I found the time too short, I know,
Too short, and much too sweet, and so
Did Harry.

The Two Goliaths
Goliath was a giant, the bully of his side,
His coat of mail was brazen, his face was
fierce with pride;
And when a shepherd stripling to challenge him was
fain,
Eleven-foot Goliath ignored him in disdain.

But David didn't trouble, his heart was cool and
glad,
Though a sling and rounded pebbles were the only
arms he had.
That slender slip of Jesse, he knew his cause was
just,
So he stood up to the bully, and rolled him in the
dust.

Those days are gone for ever, but the bully strain
survives,
Though at the time of writing one can hardly say
it thrives;
The chant of Chauvinism has become an idle yarn,
Like the 'Negligible British ' since the Battle of the
Marne.

Our German-made Goliath taunted Tommy on his size,
But the drubbing Tommy gave him has caused him

much surprise ;
And a hasty memorandum in the Teuton mind is stored
'The little British Army must never be ignored."

An Overlord

Here's a prominent person
I must write a verse on
His ways are so strictly impartial,
His power is great,
His word carries weight
In matters domestic and martial.
He never takes sides,
But rough-shod he rides
Over General French and the Kaiser;
Party spirit he shuns,
He hinders the Huns
And makes Tommy sadder and wiser.

When in genial mood
He's so kindly and good
You'd never believe he could vary.
But when out for a grumble
He's rough to your humble
And equally rude to Queen Mary.
Entente and Alliance
Endure his defiance
In mute resignation together.
His name is suppressed,
But you'll doubtless have guessed
That by trade he's the Clerk of the Weather.

April Antidotes

In the nonage of the year,
When anemones appear,
And the buffets of the breeze are soft as silk,
When each sparrow spars and heckles,
I begin to think of freckles,
And of bi-chloride of mercury and milk.

When the silver slanting shower
Hangs the almond-blossom bower
With a fringe of diamond dew and crystal link,
When the azure brooklet dimples
I begin to think of pimples,
And of benzoin and precipitated zinc.

When beneath the feathered breast
Lie the treasures of the nest,

When the sap begins to turn the birches red ;
When the lambs grow energetic
I apply a new cosmetic
Made of potash, camphor, glycerine and lead.

Then I care not if it snows,
I've a powder for the nose,
And a veil of chiffon warranted to cling ;
While my armour on I buckle,
I acknowledge with a chuckle
I'm hermetically sealed against the Spring.

The Outpost
The dying sunset's slanting rays
Incarnadine the soldier's deed,
His sturdy countenance betrays
The bull-dog breed.

Not his to shun the stubborn fight,
The struggle against cruel odds.
Alone, unaided 'tis a sight
For men and gods.

And now his back is bowed and bent,
Now stooping, now erect he stands,
And now the red life blood is sprent
From both his hands.

He takes his enemies on trust
As one who sees and yet is blind,
For every mutilating thrust
Comes from behind.

'Tis done ! The dying sun has gone,
But triumph fills the soldier's breast.
He's sewn his back brace button on
While fully dressed.

To A Taube
Above the valley, rich and fair,
On flashing pinions, glittering, gay,
You hover in the upper air,
A bird of prey.

Snarling across the empty blue
You curve and skim, you dip and soar,
A dove in flight and shape and hue
The dove of war.

Above the soldier and the slain,
An armoured bird, you hang on high,
Directed by a human brain,
A human eye.

A thirsty hunter out for blood
Drinking adventure to the dregs
Where hidden camps the country stud
You drop your eggs.

Thus, man, who reasons and invents,
Has inconsistently designed
The conquest of the elements
To kill his kind.

A Sing-Song
I. THE COMMAND

To his crack army corps, 'twas the Kaiser who spoke :
By Bavarians bold must the British be broke.
'Tis the hope of my heart they may meet you but once,
To let the world see how Meinheer Atkins runs.
So fill up your cups with Bavarian beer,
Of contemptible armies the road you must clear.
Then go for the British and show me some sport
Wipe them out of existence, and send your report.'

II. THE REPORT

' We met,
'Twas in a crowd,
And we thought they would shun us.
We stormed ;
They would not budge,
But they started to gun us.

They charged,
We did not wait,
There was no time to potter.
We thought
We were hot stuff,
But the Tommies were hotter.

We're nabbed ;
They've got us tight,
And we're sadder and wiser,
And you
Are the cause
Of this anguish, my Kaiser.'

An Anzac Cap

It hangs on the wall, a trifle battered,
The wire is warped and the lining tattered.
And the leather inside shows speakingly how
It's been wet with the sweat of a soldier's brow.

Month after month, through that fierce campaign
The bitterest fight that was fought in vain
It was jammed on an Anzac's lean, brown poll,
As he pierced his way to a glimpse of goal.

Furlong by furlong, aye, inch by inch,
From the sniping shot to the cold-steel, clinch-
Fists, "rough-housing," any old tools
He got there each time by "Rafferty rules."

Till a shell, with his name on, gave him a call
And that is the tale of the cap on the wall,
But the sequel, though strange, is an equally true one
Its owner, thank God, is now wearing a new one.

Anzac

We know that you're sportsmen, with reason,
At footer and cricket you're crack;
I haven't forgotten the season
When we curled up before the "All Blacks."
In the matter of wielding the "willow,"
We own, to our cost, that you're it,
The "ashes" you've borne o'er the billow
Though they're home again now, for a bit.

There are weightier matters to settle
To-day, amid bullets and shells;
And the world stands amazed at the mettle
You've shown in the farDardanelles.
The marvellous feat of your landing
Your exploits by field and by deed,
Your charges that brooked no withstanding,
Though you poured out the best of your blood.

You left your snug homesteads "down under";
The prosperous life of your land,
And staggered the Turks with your thunder,
To give the Old Country a hand.
For dare-devil work we may book you,
You're ready and keen to get to it.
If a job is impossible, look you,
The boys from "down under" will do it

An Anzac Poem
Why do we cheer those brown-faced boys with pride,
Why do dense crowds press round on every side,
Why do we throw them flowers, our hearts aglow?
Well—turn a minute to three years ago.

A moonlit beach—a cliff of scrub and bush
The creeping, crowded boats—a breathless hush,
A cranch of keels —a leap, a shallow splash
And then Inferno, thunder, blaze and crash.

"Straight as a bayonet"—riddled where they fell;
Hacking the wire, across that strip of Hell;
Those untried heroes—husky and blood-drenched
Hurled back the Turkish outposts —and entrenched!

The thing that was impossible was done!
From the beginning thus have Britons won.
So, year by year, in words of fire and gold,
The Anzacs' glorious landing shall be told

The K A Boys
Dr-rud dr-rud dr-rud dr-rud
Kitchener's Army on the march
Through Marylebone and Marble Arch,
Men in motley, so to speak,
Been in training about a week,
Swinging easy, toe and heel,
Game and gay, and keen as steel.

Dr-rud dr-rud dr-rud dr-rud
Norfolk jackets, city suits,
Some in shoes and some in boots;
Clerk and sportsman, tough and nut,
Reach-me-downs and Bond-Street cut;
Typical kit of every kind,
To show the life they've left behind.

Dr-rud dr-rud dr-rud dr-rud
Marching by at an easy pace,
The great adventure in every face.
Raw if you like, but full of grit,
Snatching the chance to do their bit.
Oh, I want to cheer and I want to cry
When Kitchener's Boys go marching by.

Another Pair Of Sleeves

Time was, not very long ago,
When Mabel's walking skirt
Trailed half a yard behind to show
How well she swept the dirt.
But 'short and sweet' are in again;
No more the grievance rankles,
For Mabel's now curtailed her train
And shows her dainty ankles.

But Mabel has a thrifty mind
To supplement her charms.
The frills that once she wore behind
She fastens on her arms.
Her sleeves are made in open bags
Like trousers in the navy;
No more she sweeps the streets, but drags
Her sleeve across the gravy.

A Sore Point
It was clear that poor Richard was out of the running,
His mortification he could not disguise.
She flirted with Edward, the company shunning,
Soul leaping to soul through their eloquent eyes.
Devotion of years had he lavished in vain,
But the luck took a turn when Ted trod on her train.

There sounded a rip as if stitches were slitting,
The lady herself was brought up with a jerk.
Ted smiled his excuses, facetiously fitting
The little mishap with a humorous quirk.
Poor innocent fool! his smile faded to gloom,
For he read in her look his immutable doom.

Her peach-blossom face wore a look so malignant
His dexterous epigram faltered and failed,
Her eye scattered lightnings forbidding, indignant,
His ardour was quenched and his countenance paled,
While she riddled his length with a fire of disdain.
From his head to his foot (on her gossamer train).

So she took Dick instead, and their days pass serenely,
He watches his feet and is careful to steer;
She sweeps o'er the carpet majestic and queenly;
He follows a yard and a half in the rear.
His duties are heavy, but perfectly plain:
To work for her, love her, and keep off her train.

The Niggers

When Sibyl sits upon the beach
With Kate and Madeline,
Dick, Tom and Jack, the swain of each,
Loll gloomily between,
With savage glances at the throng
Of stripe-bedizened figures
Who stain the breeze with strident song,
In other words the Niggers.

In vain the lovers hint or nudge,
Suggest a sail, a walk,
Their promised brides refuse to budge,
And beg them not to talk.
For Sibyl loves the corner man,
Kate drinks the Tenor's tones,
While Madeline, behind her fan,
Beams rapture on the Bones.

They whisper of 'romantic eyes,'
Of 'teeth like milky pearls,'
Perceiving through a thin disguise
A row of fallen Earls.
Jack loathes the tenor's unctuous smirks,
And Tom the corner-prattle,
And frowns defy the man that works
What Richard calls the rattle.

Their old allurements they rehearse,
Exhaust each manly wile,
But matters go from bad to worse,
They never win a smile;
Till, hitting on a way by which
To better their condition,
They black their faces, hire a pitch,
And start an opposition.

The Knitting Song
Soldier lad, on the sodden ground,
Sailor lad on the seas,
Can't you hear a little clicketty sound
Stealing across on the breeze?
It's the knitting-needles singing their song
As they twine the khaki or blue,
Thousands and thousands and thousands strong,
Tommy and Jack, for you.

Click - click - click,
How they dart and flick,
Flashing in the firelight to and fro!
Now for purl and plain,

Round and round again,
Knitting love and luck in every row.

The busy hands may be rough or white,
The fingers gouty or slim,
The careful eyes may be youthfully bright,
Or they may be weary and dim,
Lady and workgirl, young and old,
They've all got one end in view,
Knitting warm comforts against the cold,
Tommy and Jack, for you.

Knitting away by the midnight oil,
Knitting when day begins,
Lads, in the stress of your splendid toil,
Can't you hear the song of the pins?
Clicketty, click - through the wind and the foam
It's telling the boys over there
That every 'woolly' that comes from home
Brings a smile and a hope and a prayer.

Click - click - click,
How they dart and flick,
Flashing in the firelight to and fro!
Now for purl and plain,
Round and round again,
Knitting love and luck in every row.

The Longest Odds
Leonidas of Sparta, years gone by,
With but a bare three hundred of his braves,
In the ravine of famed Thermopylae
Held up the Persian army's endless waves.
Smiling, among the forest of his spears,
'Lay down your arms, the haughty Xerxes cried.
The Spartan's answer echoes down the years,
'Come here and take them!' So they fought, and died.

Horatius the odds grow longer now
With two bold friends, Lars Porsena defied.
That dauntless trio registered a vow
To hold the bridge that stemmed the Tiber's tide.
Their deed of valour makes our bosoms glow,
A deed which poets and chroniclers relate.
Three heroes held in check a bitter foe
And saved their city from a cruel fate.

One Highlander the longest odds of all
One man alone, when all the rest were slain,
Carried the Maxim through the bullet squall,

And set it spitting at the foe again.
Under its hail the Germans broke, they fled.
One man, one gun, and yet they would not stay!
Riddled with shot, his comrades found him dead.
Dead? No! That Hieland laddie lives for aye.

The Nut
He used to get, when in civilian state,
His tea and shaving water, sharp, at eight.
Then ten delicious minutes would be spent
In one last snooze of exquisite content.

That cosy nest, luxuriously sprung,
Was like a cloud 'twixt earth and heaven hung,
The eiderdown and blankets, soft and warm,
Were yet as light as spindrift in a storm.

Unparalleled contingencies since then
Have found a soldier in the citizen.
In inky tent he thrusts and coils each limb
To make his one ewe blanket cover him.

The Spartan methods of a scanty kit
May make the budding soldier hard and fit,
Yet, while he sleeps, a chilliness of spine
Breeds harassed dreams of "shun! 'and' Right incline!'

Grumble not he it's all a bit of fun.
'One blanket's better,' as he says, 'than none'
The same for him as other Tommies, but
No disrespect in future for the Nut!

[The 'Nut' referred to is Jessie Pope's son Gilbert]

The Nut's Birthday
When Gilbert's birthday came last spring,
Oh! How our brains were racked
To try to find a single thing
Our languid dear one lacked;
For, since he nestled at his ease
Upon the lap of Plenty,
Stock birthday presents failed to please
The Nut of two and twenty.
And so we bought to suit his taste
Refined and dilettante
Some ormolu, grotesquely chased;
A little bronze Baccante;
A flagon of the Stuart's reign.

A 'Corot' to content him.
Well, now his birth's come again,
And this is what we sent him.

Some candles and a bar of soap,
Cakes, peppermints and matches,
A pot of jam, some thread (like rope)
For stitching khaki patches.
These gifts our soldier write to say,
Have brought him untold riches
To celebrate his natal day
In hard-won Flander's ditches.

A Vain Appeal
[From Edwin]
Now, Angelina, put it down.
Let me entreat you not to smoke it;
You dread your Edwin's lightest frown,
Or so you say well, don't provoke it.
No No I'm serious just now,
Great weight to every word attaches;
What's that you ask me? Anyhow
To pass the matches!

You shall have chocolates to eat
Of every possible description;
Those rosy lips are much too sweet
To soil with Yankee or Egyptian.
Your smiles with trinkets I'll entice
Or silly frillies made of chiffon,
Till once again you say I'm nice
And not a griffon.

Among those violet-scented curls
The smell of stale tobacco lingers,
And oh ! to think my best of girls
Should go about with yellow fingers.
Are you aware that stain will spread
Right up your arm and past your shoulder
And ruin What was that you said?
You'll use a holder!

No, Angelina, I insist!
Come, darling .... what, you're surely joking?
You are not anxious to be kissed
You'd sooner give up me than smoking
So be it take your cigarette
And smoke it, love and homage scorning,
But suffer me, with much regret,
To say 'Good morning'!

April Antidotes

In the nonage of the year,
When anemones appear,
And the buffets of the breeze are soft as silk,
When each sparrow spars and heckles,
I begin to think of freckles,
And of bi-chloride of mercury and milk.

When the silver slanting shower
Hangs the almond-blossom bower
With a fringe of diamond dew and crystal link,
When the azure brooklet dimples
I begin to think of pimples,
And of benzoin and precipitated zinc.

When beneath the feathered breast
Lie the treasures of the nest,
When the sap begins to turn the birches red ;
When the lambs grow energetic
I apply a new cosmetic
Made of potash, camphor, glycerine and lead.

Then I care not if it snows,
I've a powder for the nose,
And a veil of chiffon warranted to cling ;
While my armour on I buckle,
I acknowledge with a chuckle
I'm hermetically sealed against the Spring.

The Lads Of The Maple Leaf

Ripe for any adventure, sturdy, loyal and game,
Quick to the call of the Mother, the young Canadians came.
Eager to show their mettle, ready to shed their blood,
They bowed their neck to the collar and trained in the Wiltshire mud;

Shipped, in the fulness of time, across to the other shore,
Heard a deep hum in the distance, the basso profundo of war,
Fretted to get to the business, chafed for the firing line;
Forward, with throbbing pulses, like pilgrims who near their shrine;

Spoiled for a fight, and got it - lurid, merciless, red
Trifled with death in the trenches, braved, and battled, and bled;
Then, at a given order, gathered together and backed
Not because they were bending, but to keep the line intact.

Four of their guns defenceless - left in the enemy's hand!
That was a bitter buffet, more than the lads could stand.
Back charged the men of the Maple, routed the jubilant Huns,

Captured a pack of Germans, and saved their beloved guns.

Ripe for any adventure, sturdy, loyal, and game,
Quick to the call of the Mother, the keen Canadians came.
Hurrah for the young Dominion! Then cheer them with heart and voice,
The Maple shall never wither! Bravo, Canada boys!

The Call Of The Congo
I go as a rule
At the coming of Yule,
To a place where the sunshine's obtrusive;
At Hydros I'm found,
Where dyspeptics abound,
And massage and physic's inclusive;

Or a shelter I grace
In some fashion-plate place
Where the giddy and frivolous throng go,
But to Fashion adieu,
If the rumour is true
They're reducing the fares on the Congo.

Each English resort
Will lack my support,
Nor do Cannes or Mentone intrigue me.
I see the same faces
At watering places,
And the places and faces fatigue me.

But I now can afford
To career like a lord
To the land of the palm and the mango;
To the Tropics I'll ship
For a cheap little trip,
A week end at warm Wango-wango.

Eluding the net
Of my usual set
And the hump that it constantly gave me,
The lies and the smirks
Of refinement that irks
In the Jellala Falls I will leave me.

In a place I will stay
That is called O-go-way,
I will shake by the hand the Obongo,
And with vigour renewed
I shall come back imbued
With the charms that are cheap on the Congo.

Captain Von Muller

A Skipper of mark was Von Muller,
The humorous naval leg-puller.
With ubiquitous ease
He raided the seas
And his bag became fuller and fuller.

Though now he is finally done, he
Had a nice little run for his money,
And his victims' distress
He would gently suppress
With words that were sweeter than honey.

The high seas brought hazards to suit him,
His laurels, not one will dispute him,
No Briton could crow
Over such a game foe
And his enemy's flag will salute him.

www.ingramcontent.com/pod-product-compliance
Lightning Source LLC
Chambersburg PA
CBHW061313040426
42444CB00010B/2615